Python Prog

The Complete Guide to Learn Python for
Data Science, AI, Machine Learning, GUI
and More With Practical Exercises and
Interview Questions

Written by Nicholas Ayden

Legal & Disclaimer

The information contained in this book and its contents is not designed to replace or take the place of any form of medical or professional advice; and is not meant to replace the need for independent medical, financial, legal or other professional advice or services, as may be required. The content and information in this book has been provided for educational and entertainment purposes only.

The content and information contained in this book has been compiled from sources deemed reliable, and it is accurate to the best of the Author's knowledge, information and belief.

However, the Author cannot guarantee its accuracy and validity and cannot be held liable for any errors and/or omissions. Further, changes are periodically made to this book as and when needed. Where appropriate and/or necessary, you must consult a professional (including but not limited to your doctor, attorney, financial advisor or such other professional advisor) before using any of the suggested remedies, techniques, or information in this book.

Upon using the contents and information contained in this book, you agree to hold harmless the Author from and against any damages, costs, and expenses, including any legal fees potentially resulting from the application of any of the information provided by this book. This disclaimer applies to any loss, damages or injury caused by the use and application, whether directly or indirectly, of any advice or information presented, whether for breach of contract, tort, negligence, personal injury, criminal intent, or under any other cause of action.

You agree to accept all risks of using the information presented inside this book.

You agree that by continuing to read this book, where appropriate and/or necessary, you shall consult a professional (including but not limited to your doctor, attorney, or financial advisor or such other advisor as needed) before using any of the suggested remedies, techniques, or information in this book.

Table of Contents

Python Programming

Chapter 1: Introduction to Python

What Is Python?

A general-purpose programming language, whose expansion and popularity is relatively recent. This is Python, a commitment to simplicity, versatility, and rapidity of development.

Python is a platform-independent and object-oriented scripting language prepared to perform any type of programming language, from Windows applications to network servers or even web pages. It is an interpreted language, which means that it is not necessary to compile with the source code to be capable to execute it with, which offers advantages such as the speed of development and inconveniences such as lower speed.

In recent years the language has become popular, thanks to several reasons such as:

- The number of libraries it contains, types of data and functions incorporated with the language itself, which helps to perform many common tasks without having to program them from scratch.

- The simplicity and speed with which the programs are created. A program in Python can have 3 to 5 lines of code less than its equivalent in Java or C.

- The number of platforms on which you can develop, such as Unix, Windows, OS/2, Mac, Amiga, and others.

- Also, Python is free, even for business purposes.

What Is Python For?

One of the main advantages of learning Python is the possibility of creating a code with great readability, which saves time and resources, which facilitates its understanding and implementation.

These factors and others that you will see later, have made Python become one of the most used programming languages. From web applications to artificial intelligence, Python uses are endless.

1- Python in Artificial Intelligence (AI)

Python is a fast, scalable, robust and open-source writing language, advantages that make Python a perfect ally for Artificial Intelligence.

It allows you to capture complex ideas with a few lines of code, which is not possible with other languages.

There are libraries such as "Keras" and "TensorFlow", which contain a lot of information about the functionalities of machine learning.

Also, there are libraries provided by Python, which are widely used in AI algorithms such as Scikitl, a free machine learning library that features several regression, classification and grouping algorithms.

2- Python in Big Data

The use of Python is widespread in data analysis and the extraction of useful information for companies.

In addition to its simplicity, which is a great advantage, Python has data processing libraries such as 'Pydoop', which are of great help to professionals, since you can write a MapReduce code in Python and process the data in the cluster HDFS

Other libraries such as "Dask" and "Pyspark" make data analysis and management even easier. Python is fast and easily scalable, features that help you generate information in real-time environments and convert that information to the languages used in Big Data.

3- Python in Data Science

Since the introduction of Python numerical engines such as 'Pandas' and 'NumPy', researchers have switched to Python from the previous language, MATLAB.

Python deals with tabular, matrix and statistical data, and even displays them with popular libraries such as «Matplotlib» and «Seaborn».

4- Python in Test Frameworks

Testing is another activity that has been changed to Python.

Python is ideal for validating ideas or products, as it has many integrated frameworks that help debug code and offer fast workflows and execution.

Testing tools such as 'Unittest', 'Pytest' and 'Nose test' make testing easier. Python also supports cross-platform tests and browsers with different frames, such as "PyTest" and "Robot."

Testing, which is usually one of the most arduous tasks, becomes something much simpler and faster.

5-Python in Web Development

Python allows you to build much more with fewer lines of code, so prototypes are created more efficiently.

The Django framework, provided by Python, is an advantage for all developers, as it can be used to create dynamic and very secure web applications.

The Python language is also used for scraping, that is, obtaining information from other websites. Applications like Instagram, Bit Bucket, Pinterest are built in such frameworks.

Python uses and applications are well beyond the aforementioned fields, from game development to data visualization, from networking to software development in general. Python applications are numerous.

If you are a developer or want to dedicate yourself to one of the fields mentioned above, we invite you to take a little of your time to finish to read this whole book. Python is one of the languages that

14

you must learn and master to work on the most cutting-edge technological projects.

Python Features

Let's see the main properties of the Python language, which are very similar to programming languages such as Java or Ruby

1- General-Purpose Language

That means that it is not aimed at a specific purpose, such as PHP, specially designed to make websites.

With Python, you can create pages without having a high knowledge (with Javascript as a powerful ally), but also make scripts or software for the Windows operating system.

There is still nothing featured for mobile devices, but you can use Kivy for this purpose.

2- It is multiparadigm

And what does that mean? Multiparadigm?

Well, although its strong is object-oriented programming (it is a high-level language), there are other programming paradigms or styles for its users, such as imperative programming (with loop sentences) or functional programming (with modules and functions).

So, if you don't know anything about objects and only know how to write code using methods, you can use Python perfectly, which in other languages do that is impossible.

3- Python is an interpreted language

When you program in Python, you do not compile the source code to machine code, but there is an interpreter that will execute the program based on the code directly.

Although this property suggests that programs may be slower, that in Python language is not
16

usually so, that facilitates the development of the following feature.

4- It is cross-platform

Unlike many languages such as visual basic, which mainly you can only do things for Windows, with Python you can use it in many devices and operating systems since interpreters have been created for Unix, Linux, Windows and Mac Os systems.

5- It is dynamic typing

When you declare a variable, it is not necessary to tell what types the data is (if it is int, string, float, etc.). The variable adapts to what you write when the program is executed.

Before this feature has always been criticized in other languages, for the optimization of memory, errors when writing code, etc. But with Python the goal is for language to help create software, not having to deal with peculiarities of the language.

Similarly, Python is strongly typed, for example, you will not be able to add numbers and text (a variable of type int with one of the type strings) because it would give an error.

6- It is object oriented

We have already said that you can apply another programming style, making object-oriented software entails a series of standard advantages, especially when reusing components thanks to inheritance and its polymorphism functions.

Python Philosophy

Very often most programmers in this language will hear someone say something related to the Python philosophy which is very similar to the Unix philosophy.

These principles were famously described by Python developer Tim Peters in Python Zen.

- Beautiful is better than ugly.

- Explicit is better than implicit.

- Simple is better than complex.

- The complex is better than complicated.

- The flat is better than nested.

- Scattered is better than dense.

- Readability counts.

- Special cases are not so special as to break the rules.

- The practical gains the pure.

- Errors should never be passed silently.

- Unless they have been silenced explicitly.

- Faced with ambiguity, rejects the temptation to guess.

- There should be one - and preferably only one - obvious way to do it.

- Although that way may not be obvious at first unless you are Dutch.

- Now it's better than ever.

- Although it is never better than now.

- If the implementation is difficult to explain, it is a bad idea.

- If the implementation is easy to explain, it may be a good idea.

- Namespaces are a great idea. Let's do more of those things!

Tim Peters, The Python Zen.

Python History And Evolution

The history of Python as a programming language begins in the late 80s and early 90s with Guido Van Rossum, a history of 29 years of development.

On a Christmas in 1989, Guido Van Rossum, who worked at the CWI (a Dutch research center), decided to start a project as a hobby giving continuity to ABC, a programming language that was developed at the CWI.

Retrieve words from a document in ABC   Retrieve words from a document in PYTHON

ABC was developed in the early 80s as an alternative to BASIC, it was designed for beginners for its ease of learning and use. His code was compact but readable.

The project did not transcend as the hardware available at the time made its use difficult. So, Van Rossum gave it a second life creating Python.

Guido Van Rossum liked the Monty Python group, for this reason, he chose the name of the language. Currently, Van Rossum continues to play the central role in deciding the direction of Python.

The versions indicated in red are considered obsolete

In 1991, Van Rossum published the version 0.9.0 code in alt.sources.

21

This version shows a module system adopted from Modula-3, a structured and modular programming language, which Guido describes as one of Python's largest programming units. For example, Python's exception model is like Modula-3's

By 1994, comp.lang.python was created, a Python discussion forum that marked a milestone in its popularity and multiplied its number of users.

Version 1.0

For this same year, Python reaches version 1.0 that included functional programming tools such as lambda, reduce, filter and map.

Tools that came to the language thanks to a Lisp hacker, a family of multiparadigm-type computer programming languages.

The last version released in CWI was Python 1.2, in 1995, Van Rossum continued his work at the Corporation for National Research (CNRI) in

Virginia, where he released several versions of the language.

For version 1.4, there are new features, many inspired by Modula-3, and also built-in support for complex numbers.

By 2000, the main Python developer team was switched to BeOpen.com to form the BeOpen Python Labs team. CNRI requested that version 1.6 be published at the time the team left CNRI.

Version 1.6 published in the CNRI includes a license substantially longer than that of the versions published in CWI. The new license included a clause stating that it was governed by the laws of Virginia.

The Free Software Foundation (FSF), a foundation created by Stallman to encourage Free Software, argued that the clause was incompatible with GNU GPL. So, they agreed to change Python to a Free Software license, which would make it compatible with GPL.

This is why Python 1.6.1 is the same as 1.6, with a couple of bug fixes and a new GPL-compatible license.

Version 2.0

Python 2.0 included the generation of lists, one of the most important features of the Haskell functional programming language. It also included a garbage collection system capable of collecting cyclic references.

In 2001, the Python Software Foundation was created, which as of Python 2.1 owns all the code, documentation and language specifications. The foundation was based on the Apache Software Foundation model.

Version 3.0

The last major Python update was in 2008 with Python 3.0 with the PEP 3000, designed to rectify fundamental flaws in language design.

"Reduce feature duplication by removing old ways of doing things"

The philosophy of Python 3.0 is the same as the previous versions, however, Python as a language has accumulated new and redundant ways of programming the same task.

Python 3.0 has emphasized eliminating duplicate constructors and modules to comply with the "have only one obvious way of doing things" rule.

The Python 3.x and Python 2.x versions were planned to coexist for several releases that were released in parallel, where Python 2.6 was released at the time with 3.0, including new features and alerts that highlight the use of tools removed in version 3.0

Similarly, 2.7 was released at the time with 3.1 and includes features of the new version, with 2.7 being the last publication in the 2.x series, which currently only receives security updates and will no longer be supported in 2020.

Python 3.0 breaks the backward compatibility of the language since Python 2.x code does not necessarily have to run in Python 3.0 without any modification..

One of the most impressive projects written in Python is the Dropbox server, (where Guido works today) that today serves millions of people. Another incredible use is by the scientific community as a tool for Machine Learning.

Finally, we leave you with a message from Guido Van Rossum. It is for all young programmers, or those who are starting to program.

Chapter 2: Basics of Python

TYPE OF DATA

The information that is processed in computer programs is represented in various ways. If you treat numerical information, you will use simple or real values or simple data. If you work logical expressions with true or false results you will use logical or Boolean data. If, on the other hand, you manipulate text you will use data of type character or string of characters (string). To represent numerical information (or even logical or text) where the data is grouped in the form of tables, such as vectors and matrices, or more complex structures, composite data types will be used.

The types of data used in the main programming languages are shown in the figure below.

Note: The character data type does not exist in Python, a simple character is represented as a character string (string).

Structures composed of languages such as C, FORTRAN, Pascal, Matlab, etc. Py: Composite structures in Python. Source: self-made.

Simple data

The elementary data is simple, also called scalars because they are indivisible objects. Simple data are characterized by having a single value associated and are of the integer, real or floating-point (float), Boolean and character type. In Python, there is no simple character data type. Although the data consists of only one letter or ASCII character it is represented as a data composed of a string of characters (string).

- *Integers*

In mathematics, the integers are the natural numbers, their negatives and zero. Examples of integers: 5, -20, 0, -104. Numbers with decimal parts are not included among the integers, such as 3.4. Integers, in most programming languages including Python, are defined with the word int. Python has an internal type function that returns the given data type:

In C ++ or Pascal 4 bytes (32 bits are used, and one bit is reserved for the sign, signed 32-bit) for standard integers (int, integer), represented in the number range:

−2147483648... 2147483647

For greater range in these languages, 8 bytes (signed 64-bit) are used, declaring them as long or int64:

−263.......263 −1

Unlike C++ or Pascal, in Python integer data is stored with "arbitrary precision", that is, the number of bytes needed to represent the integer is used. For example, the numbers 5 (binary: 101) and 200 (2^7 + 2^6 + 2^3, binary: 11001000) are represented:

The internal Python bin (N) function converts an integer to string with the equivalent binary (0b + binary). To check the wide range of values in Python, let's test a value greater than 2^{63}, such as 2^{220}

```
>>> 2**220

1684996666696914987166688442938726917102321526408785780068975640576
```

* _Real_

Unlike integers that are discrete values from one natural number to another, the continuous value numbers of the set of real numbers in Mathematics are called real or floating-point/point8, or simply float. Not all real numbers can be accurately represented in computer science because many have infinite decimal places. However, according to the level of precision, we want these numbers can be approximated well enough. The use of the IEEE 754 standard to represent real or floating-point numbers has been agreed for several decades, using scientific notation.

This notation allows you to represent numbers with a mantissa (significant digits) and an exponent separated by the letter 'e' or 'E'. For example, the number 4000 is represented by the mantissa 4 and the exponent 3, 4e3. It reads 4 times from 10 to 3. The number 0.25 is also represented as 25e-2. It is also allowed to omit the initial zero, .25 and the real number 4.0 can be entered as 4. (without the zero after the period).

Sign	Exponent	Mantista
1 Bit	11 Bits	52 Bits

Value= $(-1)^{sign} * 1.\text{Mantisa} * 2^{(Exponent-1023)}$

Thus, with 64 bits the numbers (decimals) of $\pm$ 5.0 * 10^{-324} (precision) can be represented up to $\pm$ 1.7 * 10^{308} range. The IEEE 754 standard updated in 2008 incorporates the decimal64 format that uses the decimal base to improve binary representation errors[1]. Python incorporates the Decimal function of the decimal module.

Below are several examples of real numbers, the real type (float) and a typical error with representation of floating point with binary base, in the case of the value 0.1.

---

[1] (IEEE Standards Committee, 2008

```
>>> 25e-2

0.25

>>> 4e3

4000.0

>>> type (4.)

<class 'float'>

>>> .2e2

20.0

>>> 1.1 + 2. 2 # is represented with binary
floating point error

3.3000000000000003
```

- *Booleans*

The type of data to represent logical or Boolean values in Python is bool, in Pascal and C++ they are defined as boolean and bool, respectively. Boolean data takes the value True (1 logical) or

33

False (0 logical). The Boolean name is used after George Boole, an English mathematician, proposed in the 19th century an algebraic system based on these two logical values and three logical operations: "and logical", "or logical" and negation. Examples:

```
>>> a = 3 > 2
>>> a
True
>>> type(a)
<class 'bool'>
>>> 4 > 5
False
```

- *Character*

The type of character data used in several programming languages is the scalar or indivisible element of the texts used in computer science. The

34

texts are called a character string. For example, the ASCII characters ordered from decimal value 20 to 127 are:

```
! " # $ % & ' ( ) * +, -. / 0 1 2 3 4 5 6 7 8 9:; < =
> ? @ A B

C D E F G H I J K L M N O P Q R S T U V W X
Y Z [ \] ^ _ ` a b c d

e f g h i j k l m n o p q r s t u v w x y z {|} ~
```

The order in which they are represented serves to evaluate which is greater than another, according to the numerical value in which they appear in the ASCII code. For example, 'b' is greater than 'a'.

The character type is not defined in Python. Simple characters are defined just like a text with a single letter, that is, as a string of characters (string).

```
>>> type('a')
```

```
<class 'str'>
```

It can be seen that the character 'a' in Python is of type string (str), although in other languages such as Pascal it would be of type character (char).

Composite or structured data

Composite or structured data includes data with elements of values of the same type or of different types, which are represented unified to be saved or processed.

- _Characterized string data: string_

The string data type is the basic structure for handling text, which includes alphanumeric characters and other characters of the ASCII or UTF-8 encoding. Strings in Python are defined in single (") or double ("") quotes. They can also be defined in triple quotes ("" ") when multiple lines are thrown. For example,

```
>>> 'Hi'

'Hi'

>>> b = "Wooden house"

>>> type(b)

<class 'str'>

>>> type (15)

<class 'int'>

>>> type ('15')

<class 'str'>
```

The texts 'Hi' or "Wooden house" are of type string in general in all languages. The value 15 is an integer type number (int), however, the value '15' is a string (str). If quotes (") or single quotes (') are included within a string, they may give erroneous results when these characters are used to delimit the string. You can use the character that has not been used as a delimiter within the text:

```
>>> 'She said "Cute"'

'She said "Cute"'

>>> "He doesn't know"

"He doesn't know"
```

However, in these cases you can also use the backslash character (\) that serves as an escape to add quotes or other actions within the string:

```
>>> print ('He doesn\'t know I \"will come\"')

He doesn't know I "will come"
```

The backslash character (called escape character) followed by n (\ n) indicates jump to a new line. Multiple lines can be included in a string using triple quotes "" "..." "". In this case, line ends are included. Jump to a new line can be seen when they appear on the screen with the internal print function ():

```
>>> print ('We change line \ new line')

We change line

New line

>>> "" "

Program:

Author:

Date:" ""

'\ n Program: \ n Author: \ n Date: \ n'
```

Variables and assignment action

In mathematics, variables are used to represent numerical values. A character or text is used to represent them. In mathematical calculation, a function of the type $y = f(x)$ involves two variables, x, and y.

In programming languages, it is usually required to remember or save the numerical, Boolean or text values to be used once or multiple times in the program. The variables have this task. In languages such as FORTRAN, C / C++ or Pascal, a variable is considered a container or place within the computer's RAM, with an associated name (identifier), where a value of a certain type is stored. By using computer programs, we can stick with this concept. However, in Python, the concept is somewhat different, since the variables are not a place of memory that contains a value but are associated, or refer to, a place of memory that contains that value. The values can be an integer, real, boolean, etc.

The assignment action is used to give a variable a certain value. In Python, the action of assigning values to a variable means that the variable with its given name will be associated with the value to the right of the assignment:

```
>>> a = 7
```

In Python, what happens when executing the statement or instruction a = 7 is that an object with the value 7 of type int is created first and placed in a memory location. This place of memory is called the Python object identity. Then, the action of assigning 7 to the variable a will cause this name or identifier to be associated or refers to the memory address of object 7, that is, it will have the same identity as 7. We will use the internal Python id () function to better understand this reference of the variable to the place of memory where it is 7. The id () function returns the identity or place of memory where the object is located.

Simple data objects in Python have three characteristics:

Value, type, identity

```
>>> id (7)

1449917120

>>> a = 7

>>> id(a)

1449917120

>>> b = 7

>>> id(b)

1449917120

>>> c = a

>>> id(c)

1449917120
```

Both 7, a, b or c are the same object and occupy a unique memory position. In this case, position 9 1449917120. The variable b, when assigned the same value (and object) 7, will be referred to the same position. The same if you assign variable a to

42

variable c; c will refer to the same position of 7. This makes Python handle memory more efficiently because in other languages the use of it would be tripled by having three variables with the same value. But what happens if you use the value 7.0 instead of 7?:

```
>>> x = 7.0

>>> id(x)

1722264

>>> type(x)

<class 'float'>
```

The variable x will be associated with object 7.0, with identity 1722264, of type float and value 7.0. Thus, Python objects have three characteristics: value, type and identity. As noted, the variables do not need to have their type declared before they are used, as in Pascal or C. They can even change the type throughout the program.

To better appreciate the concept of assignment in programming and differentiate it from the symmetry of the symbol = in mathematics, let's try:

```
>>> 7.0 = x

SyntaxError

>>> x = x + 3

>>> x

10.0
```

The 7.0 = x statement is a syntax error in programming, although it is valid in mathematics. But x = x + 3 would be absurd in mathematics, but in programming languages it means adding to the variable x the value 3 and then the result of that expression then assigning it to the same variable x.

Python allows multiple assignments of the type

```
>>> x, y, z = 7, 8.2, 9
```

The variable y is real of value 8.2, x is an integer of value 7 and z integer of value 9. To the right of the assignment, a compound data, a tuple in Python, has been written, which is assigned to the tuple formed by the three variables.

In summary: in Python, a variable is not stored directly in memory; an object is created (whose position in memory is called identity), and the identifier of the variable is associated with the identity of that object. The following figure shows an example of the use of variables of the same value in Python, bought with other programming languages.

Expressions and sentences

Expressions are the mechanism to make calculations and consist of combinations of values and identifiers with operators. They can include variables, data, operators, parentheses and functions that return results.

Every expression has a value that is the result of evaluating it from left to right, considering the precedents. Examples of expressions:

```
>>> 1.5*3/2

2.25

>>> 1.2*x + 3 # The value of x in the previous
example is 10.0

15.0

>>> 3 > (3.1 + 2)/3

True
```

The sentences or instructions are the basic units of the programs (also called in the slang of the programmers, codes) that produces an action, such as assigning a value to a variable, displaying a result, etc. The Python interpreter executes each statement producing the given action.

```
>>> y = x/2 + 3

>>> print(y)

8.0
```

```
>>> 1.5*3/2

2.25

>>> print (_)

2.25
```

The first sentence in the box on the left calculates the expression x / 2 + 3 and the result assigns it to the variable y. The second statement shows the value of y. But, the expression in the box on the right 1.5 * 3/2, whose calculation is not assigned to any variable, its result is saved associated with a variable called "_".

Operators

The operators are the symbols that represent the calculation actions. In addition to classical mathematical operations, logical and relationship or comparison operators are used in programming. We can classify the operators of 3 types: arithmetic operators, logical or Boolean operators, and relational operators.

Arithmetic operators

Operation	Operator	Expression	Result type
Sum	+	a+b	Integer if a and b integers;

			real if any is real
Subtraction	-	a-b	Integer if a and b integers; real if any is real
Multiplication	*	a*b	Integer if a and b integers; real if any is real
Division, a ÷ b (integer)	/	a/b	Always real
Division, integer	//	a//b	Returns the whole

			part of the quotient a ÷ b
Module, rest	%	a%b	Returns the rest of the division a ÷ b
Exponentiation, a^b	**	a**b	Integer if a and b integers; real if any is real

Examples:

```
>>> 14/4       # Integer Division
```

3.5

>>> 14 // 4   # Division, returns whole part of dividing 14 by 4

3

>>> 14% 4   # Module, returns the rest of dividing 14 by 4

2

Arithmetic operators that operate on a single operand are called unary: sign change operator - and identity + operator. For example, -4, +4, --4 equals 4.

Arithmetic operators with assignments

The action of increasing the value of a variable is very common in computer programs.

For example, in an event counter, the counter c is incremented by 1.

```
>>> c = c + 1    # the variable c is increased by 1

>>> d = d - 1    # the variable d is decremented by
1
```

Python includes statements that compact the assignment operator with any arithmetic operator. In cases of increase or decrease of a variable we have,

```
>>> c + = 1       # equals: c = c + 1

>>> x + = 0.01   # equals: x = x + 0.01

>>> d - = 2       # equals: d = d - 2
```

The other arithmetic operators (*, /, //, %, **) can also be used in this compacted form. Expressions such as increment, or other operation may also be included:

```
>>> y *= d+1                          # equals: y
= y * (d + 1)

>>> n = 7

>>> n //= 2                           # equals: n
= n // 2

>>> n

3

>>> n **= 2                           # equals: n =
n ** 2

>>> n

9
```

Operation	Operator	Expression	Equals to
Add and	+=	a += b	a = a+b

assign			
Subtract and assign	-=	a -= b	a = a-b
Multiply and assign	*=	a *= b	a = a*b
Divide and assign	/	a /= b	a = a/b
Divide and assign the integer part	//=	a //= b	a = a//b
Module and	%=	a %= b	a = a%b

assign	
Power	**=
and	a **= b a a =
assign	a**b

A	B	A or B	A and B	Not A
False	False	False	False	True
False	True	True	False	True
True	False	True	False	False
True	True	True	True	False

Equals:

A	B	A or B	A and B	Not A
0	0	0	0	1
0	1	1	0	1
1	0	1	0	0

1	1	1	1	0

For example,

```
>>> A = True
>>> type(A)
<class 'bool'>
>>> B = False
>>> A or B
True
```

The following table summarizes some logical laws useful for dealing with Boolean expressions. They can be demonstrated using the truth table on each side of equality.

not not A = A

A and True = A

A and False = False

A or False = A

A or True = True

not (not A and not B) = A or B

not (not A or not b) = A and B

Python and other languages such as C++ include logical operators on binary numbers, performed bit-by-bit. These bitwise operators perform the logical operations on the bits of the binary number equivalent to the decimal number entered. For example, 5) 10 equals 101 and 6) 10 is 110. If you make a "and logical" bit by bit you will have binary 100, which is equivalent to 4) 10. At the machine language level, the operator or exclusive (xor) is also used, which returns 1 when only one of the operands is 1. In Python, as in C++, the bit operators are.

Bit operation	Operator	Expression	Result

"y logical", and	&	5 & 6	101 and 110 -> 100, 4 decimals
"or logical", or	d|	5 | 6	101 or 110 -> 111, 7 decimals
or exclusive", or	^	5 ^ 6	101 xor 110 -> 011, 3 decimals
Complement, not	~	~x	switch 0's by 1's and 1's by 0's. Equals to -x -1
Left shift	<<	x << n	Returns x with bits shifted n places to the left. Equivalent to x *2 **n
Right shift	>>	x >> n	Returns x with bits

			shifted n places to the right. Equivalent to x // 2 ** n

Relational Operators (comparison)

They are used to compare 2 expressions or values and the result is always true or false, that is, Boolean.

Relational Operators

Math	In Python	Meaning	Example	Result
=	= =	Equal to	'a' == 'b'	False
≠	!=	Different to	'b' != 'B'	True
<	<	Smaller than	7 < 3	False
>	>	Greater than	7 > 3	True
≤	<=	Smaller	7 <= 7	True

		than or equal to		
≥	>=	Greater than or equal	7 >= 3	True

In the following example we will use the relational operators to check that the measured temperature, which we will assign to the variable temp, is between 37 and 42 °C, inclusive.

```
>>> temp = 38 # measured temperature

>>> (temp >= 37) and (temp <= 42)

True
```

The expression (temp> = 37) and (temp <= 42) can go without parentheses since the relational operators have a higher priority or precedence than the Booleans. Python has the characteristic that this type of expression can be written as in mathematical notation: 37 <= temp <= 42.

Expressions of the type a <b <c in Python mean (a <b) and (b <c), which improves the readability of language.

The characters of the alphabet (without the ñ) that belong to the ASCII table are ordered. The lower-case letters of the decimal equivalent binary 97 to 122 and the upper-case letters from 65 to 90. Although in Python the characters are of type string, we can compare characters and their True or False result will be given according to their ASCII position. For example, 'b'> 'a' will return True. Similarly, 'B'> 'a' will return False.

In the following exercise we will look for an expression that is true when, given a variable car, this is a symbol of the alphabet:

```
>>> car = 'q'
>>> (car >= 'a') and (car <= 'z') or (car >= 'A') and (car <= 'Z')
True
```

```
>>> # Equals to

>>> 'a' <= car <= 'z' or 'A' <= car <= 'Z'

True

>>> car = '&'

>>> 'a' <= car <= 'z' or 'A' <= car <= 'Z'

False
```

The result can be assigned to a Boolean variable:

```
>>> is_ letter = 'a' <= car <= 'z' or 'A' <= car <= 'Z'

>>> is_ letter

False
```

In most languages, including Python, the Boolean value True (1 logical) is greater than False (0 logical):

```
>>> True > False
```

```
True
```

Use of functions. Internal and module functions.

In various examples of programs, people use internal functions and functions of the mathematics module (math) and of which it generates random values. Among the functions already applied are:

Internal Function	Returns
Type	datatype
Id	Identity or memory location
Bin	binary string equivalent to the given integer
int, float, str	integer, real, string of the given value
Input	string of the text read from the keyboard
Print	
Abs	

round	Values to print on screen
	absolute value of a number
	round a real to the specified decimals

Math module

Pi	π value (not function)
Sqrt	square root of a number

Random module

randint	random integer in the given range

In mathematics a function returns a result depending on each value of its independent variable (s). For example: f (x) = 3x2 + 1 calculates, for x = 2, the value f (2) = 13;

f2 (x, y) = x2 + y2 calculates f (2.2) = 8; f (x) = $\sqrt{x}$ calculates f (9) = 3. The functions that return results in the programming languages behave similarly.

In the context of computer languages, a function is an instruction or a block of instructions that perform a calculation or a task, and that has an identifier as a name (identifier like variables). Of the previously used functions their names (identifiers) are type, int, abs, sqrt, round, etc. In the first example of data type we already use the call to a function (it is also said to invoke the function):

```
>>> type (7)

<class 'int'>
```

The name of the function is type and, in this case, the value 7 is its argument. The arguments are the values that we pass to the functions. Example:

```
from math import sqrt

x = abs (-9) + 3

y = sqrt(x)
```

```
print ('Square of',x, '=',y)
```

First, the sqrt function of the math module must be imported (abs does not need to be imported as it is an internal function). What is between the parentheses of abs and sqrt (the value -9 and the variable x, respectively) is the argument of the function. These functions return a value (return value) after being called. The abs function is called within an arithmetic expression, the value that it returns happens to replace it in the expression and is added to 3. Then, this new value is assigned to the variable x. Care must be taken that the type of data returned by the function is compatible with the operation to be performed. The arguments of the functions may be expressions, including expressions that include calls to other functions, as noted below,

```
y = sqrt (4 + x**2)

z = sqrt(abs (-40))
```

The round or randint functions require two arguments and return a value:

```
from random import randint

n = randint(10, 100)/3.2567

print (n, round(n,2))
```

Below is a list of some functions and values of the math (math) and random (of random values) modules.

Math module	Returns
Pi	value π = 3.141592653589793
e	value e = 2.718281828459045
ceil(x)	integer greater than x, towards ∞
floor(x)	integer less than x, toward -∞
trunc(x)	round to 0
factorial(x)	x!
exp(x)	former
log(x)	natural logarithm (base e), ln (x)

log10(x)	base 10 logarithm
sqrt(x)	square root of x
sin(x),	sine, cosine, tangent of x
cos(x), tan(x)	
degrees(x)	angle x of radians to degrees
	angle x of degrees to radians

The use of module functions can be done in 2 ways. So far, we have imported the function or value we need and apply it directly in the instruction. We can also import multiple module functions:

```
from math import sqrt, log10

x = sqrt (10)

dB = log10(x/2)
```

Alternatively, you can import the math module and use the separate module functions with a dot:

```
import math

x = math. sqrt (10)
```

```
dB = math.log10(x/2)
```

In this case, the module name can be abbreviated:

```
import math as m

x = m. sqrt (10)

dB = m.log10(x/2)
```

Python Programming

Chapter 3: Data Structures & Object-Oriented Python

For most of the examples, we have used simple data, which has a single value associated with it: an integer, a real or a Boolean. They are scalar objects because they are indivisible, that is, they do not have an accessible internal structure. We have also introduced composite data such as text or string of characters, represented by strings, as well as sequences in the form of lists that we use to cycle through elements in iterative compositions for. These types of data are not scalar because they can be divided into elements and accessed, they are structured data.

Structured or composite data contains elements, which can be simple data or other composite data. We remember that both simple and compound data in Python are treated as an object.

The elements can all be of the same type, such as strings containing characters, and in this case, they are called homogeneous structured data. Other languages (C/C ++, Matlab, Pascal) have homogeneous structures such as the array (array or table), very useful for operations with vectors or matrices. The standard Python does not have a structure such as an array of C or Pascal although the numerical Python library (NumPy) 20 does include these options.

In Python, the composite or structured data can be classified into two groups, according to the characteristic of whether or not their elements can be changed, reduced or expanded: <u>structured data mutable and immutable</u>.

Immutable structured data (static)

Immutable structured data, also called static or fixed values/size, are characterized in that the elements of their sequence cannot be changed or deleted. Nor can new elements be added to the data structure. If you want to modify this type of data, use the resource to create new value. In Python, we have as immutable structured data the character strings (string) and the tuples (tuple), as data streams, and the frozen sets (frozenset).

Character string

Strings, already introduced in the second chapter, are a sequence of characters of any type (letters, numbers, special characters; any Unicode character) that form an object of Python.

Indexing or access and sequence length

The elements (characters) of the string (or of any sequence) can be accessed through an index that is placed in square brackets, [index] and tells what position the element is inside the string.

For example,

```
>>> s = 'wooden house'

>>> letter_1 = s [0]
```

```
>>> long = len (s)

>>> last_ letter = s [long-1] # alternative: s [-1]

>>> print (letter_1, last_ letter, long)

c to 12
```

The value 'wooden house' is a string type object, which includes a sequence of 12 characters. This value is assigned to the variable s, which refers to the same object. We access the first element with the index 0 (letter_1 = s [0]). As we indicated in the introduction of the lists, remember that in Python the first element of the sequences is at position 0 when indexed (accessed). To calculate the number of elements, or length, of the sequence of structured data we use the internal function len (). The chain has 12 elements and its last element is in position 11 (length - 1) or -1.

W	o	o	d	e	n		h	o	u	s	e
0	1	2	3	4	5	6	7	8	9	10	1

											1
-	-	-	-9	-8	-7	-6	-5	-4	-3	-2	-
12	11	10									1

String elements and indexes to access them (positive and negative)

An empty string can be created: s = " (two single quotes without space), len (s) = 0.

Trimming or slicing sequences and other operations

To extract a subset of elements (or segment) of a string or any sequence, the cutting operator [n: m] is used, where n is the first element to be extracted and m-1 the last.

Several examples of access to the elements and trimming segments of the string in the previous figure are presented. The comment indicates the result:

```
>>> s = 'wooden house'

>>> segm1 = s [0: 3] # segm1 <- 'woo'

>>> segm1 = s [: 3] # segm1 <- 'woo', equivalent to
the previous slice

>>> segm2 = s [8: len (s)]  # segm2 <- 'hous'

>>> segm2 = s [8:] # segm2 <- 'hous', equivalent to
the previous slice

>>> segm3 = s [0: 14: 2] # segm3 <- 'wo nhue',
slice 0:12 in 2-in-2 steps

>>> letter_u = s [-1] # letter_u <- 'e', equals access
last element

>>> letter_penu = s [-2] # letter_penu <- 's',
equivalent to penultimate access elem
```

In the cutting operator, if the first index [: m] (before the colon) is omitted, trimming starts from the first element. If the second index [n:] is omitted, it is trimmed to the end of the sequence. Negative indexes are useful for accessing the last element [-1] or last, without requiring the use of the len () function.

The other operators such as concatenate (+) or repeat (*) strings are applicable to any sequence of data,

```
>>> s1 = 'house'

>>> s2 = s1 + 'big'

>>> s2

'big house'

>>> s3 = 3 * s1 + '!'

>>> s3

'househousehouse!'
```

The in operator is considered a Boolean operator over two strings and *returns True* if the string on the left is a segment (or substring) of the one on the right. If it is not, it returns *False.* The *not* in operator returns the opposite logical result. Examples:

```
>>> s = 'wooden house'

>>> 'house' in s

True

>>> 'housewood' in s

False

>>> 'housewood' not in s

True
```

Strings are immutable

Remember that this type of data is considered immutable because we cannot change the values of its elements or change its size. If we want to do that we must create another variable (and another

78

string value before, of course). Let's see, if we want to capitalize the first letter of the string s of the previous example, it gives us an error:

```
>>> s = 'wooden house'

>>> s [0] = 'W'

Traceback (most recent call last):

  File "<stdin>", line 1, in <module>

TypeError: 'str' object does not support item assignment
```

This action of capitalizing the first letter of the string can be done automatically, as shown in the following section, but by creating a new variable.

String methods Python is an object-oriented language and the data in Python is in the objects. In object-oriented programming, objects have associated methods to manipulate their data. The methods are similar to the functions since they receive arguments and return values. Strings have methods that are their own. For example, the upper method takes a string and returns another string but with the uppercase letters.

The upper method instead of being applied to the string s = 'wooden house', as a function, upper (s), is applied in the form s.upper (). That is, a method is applied to its values. Let's look at several methods of the strings (there are methods with and without arguments):

```
>>> s = 'wooden house'

>>> sM = s.upper () # converts the letters to uppercase

>>> sM

'WOODEN HOUSE'

>>> sM.lower () # converts the letters to lowercase

'wooden house'

>>> s.capitalize () # first letter of the string in uppercase
```

'Wooden house'

>>> s.title () # first letter of each string word in uppercase

'Wooden House'

>>> i = s.find ('e') # searches the index (position) of the first string 'e'

>>> i # if it doesn't find the string it returns -1

5

>>> s.count ('a') # count how many times the element or string appears

0

>>> s.replace ('o', 'e') # replace the first string with the second

'weeden heuse'

>>> s.split ('') # part s using the string '' producing list

['wooden', 'house']

```
>>> s1 = 'Hello'

>>> s1.isupper () # True if all characters in S are
uppercase

False # False otherwise

>>> s1 [0] .isupper ()

True

>>> s1.islower () # True if all characters in S are
lowercase

False # False otherwise

>>> s1 [1] .islower ()

True
```

The above table shows a group of typical methods of string values. We solved the problem of capitalizing the first letter with the capitalize () method. The split method divides the string into segments according to the delimiter used as an argument, which in this case is the blank space. The argument '' is the default argument, so s. split

() can be used to separate words in a text. The resulting substring (words, in this case) are returned in a list with the substring as elements.

Examples

We will show a couple of examples of travel or search in a string to (i) count the number of 'to', (ii) the number of the given character or sub-string 'c1' and search for a character or substring.

```
def count (s):

    "" "Count letter a in a string

    >>> countLetter ('hot potato', 'a')

    1

    >>> countLetter ('Esplugues', 'a')

    0

    "" "

    n = 0
```

```
for c in s:

    if c == 'a':

    n = n + 1

    return n
```

Option with s.count () method

```
def count (s):

    return s.count ('a')
```

```
def count (s, c1):

    "" "Count letter or sub-string c1 in string s

    Examples:

    >>> count ('hot potato', 'a')

    1

    >>> count ('potato', 'u')
```

```
()

"" "

n = 0

for c in s:

    if c == c1:

    n =

return n
```

The search for a character or sub-string in a string can be done with the structures for, while or directly with some method of the strings. Let's look first at the classic search options with for and while.

```
def search (s, c1):

    "" "search for letter c1 in string s

    Examples:

    >>> search ('hot potato', 'a')

    True

    >>> search ('potato', 'u')

    False

    "" "

    OK = False

    for c in s:

        if c == c1:

            OK = True

            Break

    return Ok
```

```
def search (s, c1):

    "" "search for letter c1 in string s

    Examples:

    >>> search ('hot potato', 'a')

    True

    >>> search ('potato', 'u')

    False

    "" "

    OK = False

    N = len (s)

    i = 0

    while i < N and not OK:

        if s [i] == c1:

            OK = True

        i + = 1

    return OK
```

In Python we can exit the function within a loop, so the search can be:

```python
def search (s, c1):

    "" "search for letter c1 in string s

    Examples:

    >>> search ('hot potato', 'a')

    True

    >>> search ('potato', 'u')

    False

    "" "

    for c in s:

        if c == c1:

            return True

    return False
```

But this search can be done with the methods count (), find () or simply with the Boolean operator in:

```
def search (s, c1):

    "" "search for letter c1 in string s

    Examples:

    >>> search ('hot potato', 'a')

    True

    >>> search ('potato', 'u')

    False

    "" "

    return c1 in s

    #return s.count (c1)> 0

    #return s.find (c1)> = 0
```

Tuples

Tuples, like strings, are a sequence of elements arranged in a Python object. Unlike strings (elements are characters) tuples can contain elements of any type, including elements of different types. The elements are indexed the same as the strings, through an integer. The syntax of tuples is a sequence of values separated by commas. Although they are not necessary, they are usually enclosed in parentheses,

```
# Example of tuples

>>> a = 1, 2, 3

>>> to

(1, 2, 3)

>>> b = (3, 4, 5, 'a')

>>> b

(3, 4, 5, 'a')

>>> type (a)
```

```
<class 'tuple'>

>>> type (b)

<class 'tuple'>
```

The objects assigned to variables a and b are tuples type. The important thing is to include commas between the elements. For example,

```
>>> t = 'k',

>>> t

('k',)

>>> type (t)

<class 'tuple'>

>>> t2 = 'k'

>>> t2

'k'

>>> type (t2)
```

```
<class 'str'>
```

The object 'k' is a tuple, however 'k' is a string. An empty tuple can be created using parentheses without including anything: (). We can also use the internal tuple () function to convert an iterable sequence, such as a string or list, to tuple, or create an empty tuple:

```
>>> tuple ('Hello')
('H', 'e', 'l', 'l', 'o')
>>> tuple ([1, 2])
(1, 2)
>>> tuple ()
()
```

Indexing, trimming and other tuple operations

Access to tuple elements, element extraction and operations are performed analogously to strings. Let's look at several examples:

```
>>> b = (3, 4, 5, 'a')

>>> b [0]

3

>>> b [-1]

'to'

>>> b [0: 3]

(3. 4. 5)

>>> t = ('the', 'tuples', 'are', 'immutable')

>>> t [0]

'the'

>>> t [1] = 'lists'
```

```
Traceback (most recent call last):

  File "<stdin>", line 1, in <module>

TypeError: 'tuple' object does not support item
assignment
```

The static or immutable characteristic of the tuples
is observed, as are the strings. We can include
tuples within tuples and concatenate and repeat
them, such as string,

```
>>> b = (3, 4, 5, 'a')

>>> c = (b, 2)

>>> b + c

(3, 4, 5, 'a', (3, 4, 5, 'a'), 2)

>>> 3*b

(3, 4, 5, 'a', 3, 4, 5, 'a', 3, 4, 5, 'a')
```

The iterative Python for - in composition can use
any iterable sequence, including tuples:

```
>>> games = ('tennis', 'baseball', 'football',
'voleyball', 'swimming')

>>> for sport in games:

... print (sport)

tennis

baseball

football

volleyball

swimming
```

Also, as in string sequences, in tuples, you can use the operations to concatenate (+) and repeat (*) tuples and the *in* and *not* in operators of membership of elements in tuples.

Multiple assignments and functions with multiple returns

Python allows multiple assignments through tuple assignments. These actions allow a tuple of variables to the left of an assignment is assigned a tuple of values to the right of it. The condition to be fulfilled is that the number of variables of the variable tuple is equal to the number of elements of the tuple of values. Even, the object to be assigned multiple times to the variable tuple can be a string or a list, as long as the number of characters or elements is equal to the number of variables in the tuple to which the values are assigned. Let's see some examples

```
>>> a,b,c = (1,2,3)
>>> a
1
>>> type(a)
<class 'int'>
>>> d,e,f = 'xyz'
>>> d
'x'
>>> type(d)
<class 'str'>
```

n the first tuple of variables (a, b, c) the variables receive integer values. Although this object is structured type, tuple, its elements are variables of integer type. Similarly, the tuple of variables (d, e, f) each receives values of type string and its variables will be type string.

This feature of tuple assignments allows solving easily the typical problem of variable exchange, without requiring an auxiliary variable. For example, if we want to exchange the values of the variables x = 5 and y = 7, in the classical languages it would be done:

```
>>> x = 5

>>> y = 7

>>> temp = x # use of auxiliary (temporary)
variable temp

>>> x = y

>>> y = temp
```

```
>>> print (x, y)

7    5
```

With multiple assignments of tuples, the solution is direct:

```
>>> x = 5

>>> y = 7

>>> x, y = y, x

>>> print (x, y)

7    5
```

In the case of functions, they can also return multiple results that can be assigned to multiple variables with the use of tuples. Being strict, functions only return one result. But if that value is a tuple, then it can be assigned to a tuple of variables. The number of elements is required to match. Let's look at the following function as an example:

```
def myFunction (x):

    """ "

    Returns 2 values: x increased and decreased by 1

    """ "

        return x + 1, x - 1

a, b = myFunction (10)

print (a, b)

print (myFunction (20))
```

```
>>>

11  9

(21, 19)
```

The function returns a tuple of two values. In the first instruction of the main body of the program these values are assigned to the tuple with the variables a and b. Each of these variables is of the integer type and, for argument 10 of the function, they receive the values 11 and 9, respectively. These values are shown by the first print (). The second print () directly shows the tuple that the function returns.

Functions with an arbitrary number of parameters, using tuples

In the previous topic, we analyzed functions with keywords arguments. There is the option to define a function with an arbitrary (variable) number of parameters using the * operator before the parameter name. Let's look at the function of the following example and its different calls.

```
def mean (* pair):

  sum = 0

  for elem in pair:


    sum = sum + elem


  return sum / len (pair)


print (average (3, 4))


print (average (10.2, 14, 12, 9.5, 13.4, 8, 9.2))


print (average (2))
```

```
>>>
```

```
3.5

10.9

2.0
```

The function calculates the average value of the sequence of numbers that is sent as an argument to the input parameter, which expects to receive a tuple. The function can be improved to avoid dividing by 0, in case of entering an empty tuple.

Tuple Methods

As in the strings, there are methods associated with tuple type objects and lists. but only the methods: s.index (x) and s.count (x). You can also use the internal functions max and min when the tuples (or lists) are of numerical values. If the elements are strings, calculate the major or minor element, according to the position in the ASCII table of the first character. Let's see some examples,

```
a = (2, 3, 4, 5, 79, -8, 5, -4)

>>> a.index (5) # index of the first occurrence of 5
in a

3

>>> a.count (5) # total occurrences of 5 in a

2

>>> max

79

>>> min (a)

-8

>>> b = ('az', 'b', 'x')

>>> max (b)

'x'

>>> min (b)

'az'
```

Zip function

It is an iterator that operates on several iterable ones and creates tuples by adding elements of the iterable sequences (string, tuples, lists, etc.). Example,

```
def AccountElemsSamePosition(s1, s2):

    "" "tell how many equal letters are in the same position in 2

    S1 and S2 words. You can use lists or tuples

    >>>    AccountElemsSamePosition    ('Hello', 'Casting')

    3
    """ "

    counter = 0

    for c1, c2, in zip (s1, s2):

        if c1 == c2:

            counter + = 1
```

```
return counter
```

```
>>>      AccountElemsSamePosition      ('Hello',
'Goodbye')

0

>>> AccountElemsSamePosition ('Hello', 'Casting')

3
```

Frozen sets (Frozenset)

In Python, there is another group of heterogeneous structured data that try to keep a certain relationship with set theory. This data is the Set and Frozenset sets. The first ones are presented in the following section of structured mutable or dynamic data.

A frozen set (Frozenset) is a collection of unordered items that are unique and immutable. That is, it can contain numbers, string, tuples, but not lists. That they are unique elements means that they are not repeated. The Set and Frozenset are not sequences of data.

Frozen sets are immutable because they cannot be changed or removed or added. Examples of frozen data:

```
>>> FS1 = frozenset ({25, 4, 'a', 2, 25, 'house', 'a'})
>>> FS1
frozenset ({2, 'a', 4, 'house', 25})
>>> type (FS1)
<class 'frozenset'>
>>> len (FS1)
5
```

The repeated elements (25 and 'a') that we included in the frozen set were discarded.

Types of structured mutable (dynamic) data

Unlike the frozen strings, tuples and sets, the structured mutable data, also called dynamic, are characterized in that their elements can change in value and elements can be added or deleted.

In Python, we have as mutable structured data the lists, the sets (Set) and the dictionaries. The lists and sets (Set) can be considered as the mutable equivalents to the frozen tuples and sets (Frozenset), respectively.

Lists

The lists, as well as tuples and strings, are formed by a sequence of data. But unlike tuples, its elements can be modified, eliminated or increased. The elements of the lists can be simple data (numerical or Boolean), strings, tuples or other lists. Elements are indexed the same as tuples and string, through an integer. The syntax of the lists is a sequence of comma-separated values enclosed in square brackets. Examples:

```
>>> v1 = [2, 4, 6, 8, 10]

>>> type (v1)

<class 'list'>

>>> v2 = [7, 8.5, 'a', 'Hello', (2, 3), [11, 12]]

>>> v2

[7, 8, 'a', 'Hello', (2, 3), [11, 12]]

>>> games = ['tennis', 'baseball', 'football',
'voleyball', 'swimming']

>>> games

['tennis', 'baseball', 'football', 'voleyball',
'swimming']
```

The v1 list consists of integers, while v2 includes integers, reals, strings, tuples and a list as its last element. The variable games refer to a list object with 5 elements of type string. It is similar to the previously defined tuple, but its elements can be modifiable. It is a dynamic structure.

We can generate a list with a sequence of integers with the data type range (), of the form,

```
>>> v = list (range (1,11))

>>> v

[1, 2, 3, 4, 5, 6, 7, 8, 9, 10]
```

In Python versions 2.x, range () is a function that directly generates a list. However, in versions 3.x, being range () a type of data range, we have to convert it to a list with the function list (). This function also serves to convert iterable data types, such as strings or tuples to list type. You can also create an empty list. Examples:

```
>>> t = (1, 2, 3)

>>> list (t)

[1, 2, 3]

>>> s = 'Hello'

>>> list (s)
```

```
['Hi']

>>> e = list () # empty list

>>> e = [] # empty list
```

Indexing, trimming and other list operations

In the lists, access to its elements, the extraction of elements and operations are carried out in the same way as in strings and tuples. The slice operators [n: m] are also used in the lists. Let's look at several examples:

```
>>> v2 = [7, 8, 'a', 'Hello', (2,3), [11, 12]]

>>> v2 [0]

7

>>> v2 [-1]

[11, 12]
```

```
>>> v2 [-2]

(2. 3)

>>> v2 [0: 3]

[7, 8, 'a']

>>> t = ['las', 'lists', 'are', 'mutables']

>>> t [3] = 'dynamic'

>>> t

['the', 'lists', 'are', 'dynamic']

>>> len (t)

4
```

The mutability of the lists can be observed. Lists can be concatenated and repeated with the + and * operators, respectively, such as strings and tuples,

```
>>> v1 = [2, 4, 6, 8, 10]

>>> v3 = [3, 5, 7]
```

```
>>> v1 + v3

[2, 4, 6, 8, 10, 3, 5, 7]

>>> 3*v3

[3, 5, 7, 3, 5, 7, 3, 5, 7]
```

The iterative Python for - in composition has already been used with lists in the subject of iterative compositions. With the previously defined games list, we get:

```
>>> for sport in games:

... print (sport)

tennis

baseball

football

volleyball

swimming
```

In addition, as in the string and tuple sequences, the lists can be concatenated with the + operator and repeated with the * operator. Boolean operators in and not in, as in strings and tuples, evaluate whether or not an element belongs to a sequence (string, tuple or list). Examples

```
>>> v2 = [7, 8, 'a', 'Hello', (2,3), [11, 12]]

>>> 8 in v2

True

>>> 'Hello' in v2

True

>>> 'HELLO' not in v2

True
```

Objects, values and references

The operator is available in Python that indicates whether two variables are referred to the same object or not. If we execute the instructions.

```
>>> a = 'house'

>>> b = 'house'

>>> id (a)

123917904

>>> id (b)

123917904

>>> a is b

True
```

You can see that both variables a and b are referred to the same object, which has a 'house' value and occupies the memory position 123917904 (this position is arbitrary). The instruction a is b is true.

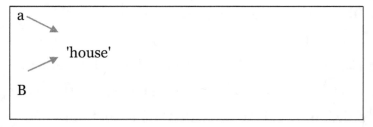

In string data types, being immutable, Python creates only one object per memory economy and both variables are referred to the same object. However, with the lists, being mutable, although two lists with the same values are formed, Python creates two objects, which occupy different memory locations:

```
>>> a = [1, 2, 3]

>>> b = [1, 2, 3]

>>> id(a)

123921992

>>> id(b)

123923656

>>> a is b

False
```

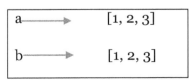

The lists assigned to variables a and b, although with the same value, are different objects. But you have to be careful with the variable assignments to the same mutable object. In the following example, when copying a variable, no other object is created, but copying refers to the same object:

```
>>> a = [1, 2, 3]
>>> b = a
>>> id(b)                    # a and b --> [1, 2, 3]
123921992
>>> a is b
True
```

It can be said that the variable b is an alias of a and that they are referenced. Therefore, if we modify or add a value to the object [1, 2, 3], through one of the variables, then we modify the other. Let's see

```
>>> b[0] = 15

>>> a

[15, 2, 3]
```

This effect can give unexpected results if not handled carefully. However, this property is used to pass parameters by reference in functions that behave as a procedure. If we want to copy one variable from another, we have the copy method, which will be presented below.

Object-oriented programming with Python

Python allows several programming paradigms, including object-oriented programming (OOP). The OOP is a way of structuring the code that makes it especially effective by organizing and reusing code, although its abstract nature makes it not very intuitive when it starts.

Object-oriented programming in Python is optional and so far, we have not used it directly, although indirectly we have done so from the beginning. Although its biggest advantage appears with long and more complex programs, it is very useful to understand how POO works since this is how Python works internally.

The basic idea is simple. If we have a more complex type of data than we have seen so far as lists or dictionaries and we want to create a new type of data with particular properties, we can define it with a class, something similar to a def function. Suppose we want to create a type of data called Star (Star), which to begin with will only have one name, we can write:

```python
# Let's create star.py

class Star(object):

    """Class for stars"""

    def __init__(self, name):
```

```
    self.name = name

  # Special method called when doing print

  def __str__(self):

    return "Stars {}".format(self.name)
```

The class has a special main function __init__ () that builds the element of the Star class (called an object) and is executed when it creates a new object or instance of that class; we have put name as the only mandatory parameter, but it does not have to have any.

The mysterious self-variable with which each function begins (called methods on objects), refers to the specific object we are creating, this will be clearer with an example. Now we can create Star type objects:

Star.py library that includes the Star import star class

\# New instance (object) of Star, with a parameter (the name), mandatory star1 = *star.Star* («*Altair*»)

\# What returns when printing the object, according to the method __*str*__ print (*star1*) \# Star Altair

print (*star1.name*) \# Altair

When creating the object with name star1, which in the class definition we call self, we have a new data type with the name property. Now we can add some methods that can be applied to the Star object:

```
class Star:

    "" "Star class

    Example classes with Python

    File: star.py

    """ "

    # Total number of stars
```

```
num_stars = 0

def __init__ (self, name):

    self.name = name

    Star.num_stars + = 1

def set_mag (self, mag):

    self.mag = mag

def set_pair (self, pair):

    "" "Assigns parallax in arc seconds" ""

    self.pair = pair

def get_mag (self):

    print "The magnitude of {} of {}". format
(self.name, self.mag)

def get_dist (self):

    "" "Calculate the distance in parsec from the
parallax" ""

    print "The distance of {} is {: .2f} pc" .format
(self.name, 1 / self.par)
```

```
def get_stars_number (self):

    print "Total number of stars: {}". format
(Star.num_stars)
```

Now we can do more things a Star object:

```
import star

# I create a star instance

altair = star.Star ('Altair')

altair.name

# Returns 'Altair'

altair.set_pair (0.195)

altair.get_stars_number ()

# Returns: Total number of stars: 1

# I use a general class method

star.pc2ly (5.13)

# Returns: 16.73406
```

```
altair.get_dist ()

# Returns: The distance of Altair is 5.13 pc

# I create another star instance

other = star.Star ('Vega')

otro.get_stars_number ()

# Returns: Total number of stars: 2

altair.get_stars_number ()

# Returns: Total number of stars: 2
```

Is not all this familiar? It is similar to the methods and properties of Python elements such as strings or lists, which are also objects defined in classes with their methods.

Objects have an interesting property called inheritance that allows you to reuse properties of other objects. Suppose we are interested in a particular type of star called a white dwarf, which are Star stars with some special properties, so we will need all the properties of the Star object and some new ones that we will add:

```
class WBStar (Star):

    "" "Class for White Dwarfs (WD)" ""

    def __init__ (self, name, type):

        "" "WD type: dA, dB, dC, dO, dZ, dQ" ""

        self.name = name

        self.type = type

        Star.num_stars + = 1

    def get_type (self):

        return self.type

    def __str__ (self):

        return "White Dwarf {} of type {}". format
(self.name, self.type)
```

Now, as a class parameter, instead of using an object to create a new object, we have set Star to inherit the properties of that class. Thus, when creating a WDStar object we are creating a different object, with all the Star properties and methods and a new property called type. We also overwrite the result when printing with print defining the special method __str__.

As we can see, the methods, which are the functions associated with the objects, only apply to them. If in our file the class, which we have called *star.py* and that now contains the *Star* and *WDStar* classes, we add a normal function, this can be used as usual:

```
class Star (Star):

    ...

class WBStar (Star):

    ...

def pc2ly (dist):
```

```
    "" "Converts parsec to many years" ""

    return dist * 3,262
```

And as always:

```
import star

# Convert parsecs into light years

distance_ly = Star.pc2ly (10.0)
```

Chapter 4: Conditionals, Iterables & Regex in Python

The control structures are if ... elif ... else ...: These constructions allow conditioning the execution of one or more sentence blocks to the fulfillment of one or more conditions.

Conditional statements: if ...

The if ... control structure allows a program to execute instructions when a condition is met. "If" means "yes" (condition)

Conditional statement syntax if ...

The syntax of the if construct is as follows:

```
if condition:

    here are the orders that are executed if the
```

> condition is true
>
> and that can occupy several lines

The execution of this construction is as follows:

- The condition is always evaluated.

- If the result is True, the statement block is executed

- If the result is False, the sentence block is not executed.

The first line contains the condition to evaluate and is a logical expression. This line must always end with a colon (:).

Next comes the block of orders that are executed when the condition is met (that is when the condition is true). It is important to note that this block must be indented since Python uses the indentation to recognize the lines that form an instruction block. The bleeding that is usually used in Python is four spaces, but more or less spaces can be used. When writing two points (:) at the end of a line, the editor will automatically bleed the following lines. To finish a block, just go back to the beginning of the line.

Flowchart that shows the execution of an "if" statement

Sample programs with conditional statements if ...

Let's see an example. The following program asks the user for a positive number and stores the response in the "number" variable. Then check if the number is negative. If it is, the program warns that that was not what was requested. Finally, the program always prints the value entered by the user. Below you can see two step-by-step executions of that program. In the first one, the user writes a negative value and in the second the user writes a positive value:

Example of "if" ... 1

```
number = int(input("Enter a positive number: "))

if number < 0:

    print("¡I told you to write a positive number!")

print(f" You have written the number {number}")
```

Example of "if" ... 2

```
number = int(input("Enter a positive number: "))

if number < 0:

    print("¡I told you to write a positive number!")

print(f"You have written the number {number}")
```

Forks: if ... else ...

The if ... else ... control structure allows a program to execute instructions when a condition is met and other instructions when that condition is not met. "If" means "yes" (condition) and "else" means "yes no". The order in Python is written like this:

130

The syntax of the if ... else ... construct is as follows:

```
if condition:

    here are the orders that are executed if the
condition is true

    and that can occupy several lines
else:

    and here are the orders that are executed if the
condition is

    false and that can also occupy several lines
```

The execution of this construction is as follows:

- The condition is always evaluated.

- If the result is True, only sentence block 1 is executed

- If the result is False, the only block of sentence 2 is executed.

The first line contains the condition to evaluate. This line must always end with a colon (:).

Next comes the block of orders that are executed when the condition is met (that is when the condition is true). It is important to note that this block must be indented since Python uses the indentation to recognize the lines that form an instruction block. The bleeding that is usually used in Python is four spaces, but more or less spaces can be used. When you write two dots (:) at the end of a line, IDLE will automatically bleed the following lines. To finish a block, just go back to the beginning of the line.

Next comes the line with the else command, which tells Python that the block that comes next must be executed when the condition is not met (that is when it is false). This line must also always end with a colon (:). The line with the else command must not include anything other than the else and the colon.

In the last place is the bleeding instruction block that corresponds to the else.

Flowchart of the conditional statement if ... else ...

The following flowchart shows the execution of an if ... else ... statement

Sample programs with conditional statements if ... else ...

Let's see an example. The following program asks the user for age and stores the answer in the "age" variable. Then check if the age is less than 18 years. If this comparison is true, the program writes that it is a minor and if it is false write that it is of legal age. Finally, the program always says goodbye, since the last instruction is out of any block and therefore is always executed. Below you can see two step-by-step executions of that program:

Example of "if" ... "else" ... 1

```
age = int(input("How old are you? "))

if age < 18:

   print("Are you a minor")

else:

   print("Are you of legal age")

print("iGoodbye!")
```

Example of "if" ... "else" ... 2

```
age = int(input("How old are you? "))

if age < 18:

   print("Are you minor")

else:

   print("Are you of legal age")

print("iGoodbye!")
```

Although it is not advisable, instead of an "if ... else" block you could write a program with two "if" blocks ...

```
age = int(input("How old are you? "))

if age < 18:

    print("Are you minor")

if age>= 18:

    print("Are you of legal age")

print("iGoodbye!")
```

It is better not to do so for two reasons:

by putting two "if" blocks, we are forcing Python to always evaluate the two conditions, while in an "if ... else" block only one condition is evaluated. In a simple program, the difference is not noticeable, but in programs that run many comparisons, the impact can be noticeable.

Using else we save writing a condition (also, writing the condition we can be wrong, but writing else not).

If for any reason you do not want to execute any order in any of the blocks, the order block must contain at least the pass order (this order tells Python that it does not have to do anything).

```
age = int(input("How old are you? "))

if age < 120:

    pass

else:

    print("¡I don't believe it!")

print(f" You say that you have {age} years.")
```

Obviously, this program could be simplified by changing inequality. It was just an example to show how the pass order is used.

```
age = int(input("How old are you? "))

if age>= 120:

    print("¡I don't believe it!")

print(f'you say that you have {age} years.")
```

More than two alternatives: if ... elif ... else ...

The if ... else ... construct can be extended by adding the elif instruction:

The if ... elif ... else ... control structure allows you to chain several conditions. elif is a contraction of else if. The order in Python is written like this:

Conditional statement syntax if ... elif ... else ...

The syntax of the if ... elif ... else ... construct is as follows:

```
if condition_1:

    block 1

elif condition_2:

    Block 2

else:

    block 3
```

- If condition 1 is met, block 1 is executed

- If condition 1 is not met but condition 2 is met, block 2 is executed

- If neither condition 1 nor condition 2 is met, block 3 is executed.

This structure is equivalent to the following nested if ... else ... structure:

```
if condition_1:

    block 1

else:

    if condition_2:

        Block 2

    else:

        block 3
```

You can write as many elif blocks as necessary. The else block (which is optional) is executed if none of the above conditions is met.

Flowchart of the conditional statement if ... elif ... else ...

In the structures if ... elif ... else ... the order in which the cases are written is important and, often, the conditions can be simplified by properly ordering the cases.

We can distinguish two types of situations:

1- When the cases are mutually exclusive

Consider a program that asks for age and depending on the value received gives a different message. We can distinguish, for example, three situations:

- if the value is negative, it is an error

- if the value is between 0 and 17, it is a minor

- if the value is greater than or equal to 18, it is a minor

Cases are mutually exclusive since a value can only be in one of the cases.

A possible program is as follows:

```
age = int(input("How old are you? "))
if age >= 18:
    print("Are you of legal age")
elif age < 0:
    print("You cannot have a negative age ")
else:
    print("You are a minor ")
```

The previous program works correctly, but the cases are messy. It is better to write them in order, to make sure we don't forget any of the possible situations. For example, we could write them from minor to older, although that forces us to write other conditions:

```
age = int(input("How old are you? "))
```

```
if age < 0:
    print("You cannot have a negative age")
elif age >= 0 and age < 18:
    print("Are you a minor")
else:
    print("Are you legal age")
```

In the previous program, comparisons can be simplified:

```
age = int(input("How old are you? "))
if age < 0:
    print("You cannot have a negative age")
elif age < 18:
    print("Are you a minor")
else:
    print("Are you of legal age")
```

These two programs are equivalent because in an "if ... elif .. else" structure when one of the Python comparisons is met, it no longer evaluates the following conditions. In this case, if the program has to check the second comparison (that of the elif), it is because the first one has not been fulfilled (that of the if). And if the first one has not been met, it is that age is greater than 0, so it is not necessary to check it in the second condition.

But you have to be careful, because if the cases of the previous program are ordered backward while maintaining the conditions, the program would not work as expected, since writing a negative value would show the message "Are you a minor".

```python
# This program does not work properly

age = int (input ("How old are you?"))

if age <18:

    print ("Are you a minor")

elif age <0:

    print ("You cannot have a negative age")

else:

    print ("Are you of legal age")
```

2-When some cases include others

Consider a program that asks for a value and tells us:

- if it is a multiple of two,

- if it is a multiple of four (and two)

- if it is not a multiple of two

Note: The value 0 will be considered a multiple of 4 and 2.

The cases are not mutually exclusive, since the multiples of four are also multiples of two.

The following program would not be correct:

```python
# This program does not work properly

number = int (input ("Enter a number:"))

if number% 2 == 0:

    print (f "{number} is a multiple of two")

elif number% 4 == 0:
```

```
    print (f "{number} is a multiple of four and two")

else:

    print (f "{number} is not a multiple of two")
```

The error of this program is that if number meets the second condition, it also meets the first. That is, if number is a multiple of four, as it is also a multiple of two, it meets the first condition and the program executes the first block of instructions, without checking the rest of the conditions.

One way to correct that error is to add in the first condition (if) that the number is not a multiple of four.

```
number = int (input ("Enter a number:"))

if number% 2 == 0 and number% 4! = 0:

    print (f "{number} is a multiple of two")

elif number% 4 == 0:
```

```
    print (f "{number} is a multiple of four and two")

else:

    print (f "{number} is not a multiple of two")
```

The following program could also have been written:

```
number = int (input ("Enter a number:"))

if number% 2 == 0 and number% 4! = 0:

    print (f "{number} is a multiple of two")

elif number% 2 == 0:

    print (f "{number} is a multiple of four and
two")

else:

    print (f "{number} is not a multiple of two")
```

This program works because the multiples of four are also multiples of two and the program only evaluates the second condition (elif's) if the first one has not been met.

But we can still simplify the program further, ordering the cases differently:

```
number = int (input ("Enter a number:"))

if number% 4 == 0:

    print (f "{number} is a multiple of four and two")

elif number% 2 == 0:

    print (f "{number} is a multiple of two")

else:

    print (f "{number} is not a multiple of two")
```

This program works correctly because although the second condition (elif's) does not distinguish between multiples of two and four, if number is a multiple of four, the program fails to evaluate the second condition because the first one is met (the one of if).

In general, the order that makes it easier to simplify the expressions is usually to consider the particular cases first and then the general cases.

If the if ... elif ... conditions cover all possibilities, the else block may not be written:

```
number = int (input ("Enter a number:"))

if number> = 0:

    print ("You have written a positive number")

elif number <0:

    print ("You have written a negative number")
```

But it is more common to replace the last elif block ... with an else block:

```
number = int (input ("Enter a number:"))

if number> = 0:
```

```
    print ("You have written a positive number")

else:

    print ("You have written a negative number")
```

Non-Boolean Conditions

Since any variable can be interpreted as a Boolean variable, if the condition is a comparison with zero, we can skip the comparison.

For example, the following program:

```
number = int (input ("Enter a number:"))

if number% 2! = 0:

    print (f "{number} is odd")

else:

    print (f "{number} is even")
```

You could write skipping the comparison:

```
number = int (input ("Enter a number:"))

if number% 2:

    print (f "{number} is odd")

else:

    print (f "{number} is even")
```

In this program, if the number is odd, number% 2 results in 1. And since the Boolean value of a nonzero number is True (that is, bool (1) is True), the condition would be met.

If the comparison is an equality, the not operator can be used. For example, the following program:

```
number = int (input ("Enter a number:"))

if number% 2 == 0:

    print (f "{number} is even")

else:

    print (f "{number} is odd")
```

You could write skipping the comparison:

```
number = int (input ("Enter a number:"))

if not number% 2:

    print (f "{number} is even")

else:

    print (f "{number} is odd")
```

In this program, if the number is even, number% 2 results in 0. The Boolean value of zero is False (that is, bool (0) is False), but by refusing to not, the condition would be met (already that not False is True.

When learning to program, this notation can be a bit cryptic, so it is recommended to start writing the complete comparisons. Later, when you have become familiar with logical expressions, it will be more natural for you to use it.

Regex in Python

regex = r '[a-z] + -? [a-z] +'

The above expression will consider valid any string that begins with one or more letters ([az] +), followed by a hyphen, which is optional, that is, it may or may not appear in the string (-?) Followed again by one or more more character from a to z, in lower case.

Some example cases are as follows:

Valid examples:

```
print   re.findall(regexp,"well-liked")   ==   ["well-liked"]

#>>> True

print re.findall(regexp,"html") == ["html"]

#>>> True
```

Invalid examples:

```
print re.findall(regexp,"a-b-c") != ["a-b-c"]
#>>> True
print re.findall(regexp,"a--b") != ["a--b"]
#>>> True
```

The first expression of the invalid examples is not correct since the second indent is not expected by the regular expression, in the second example, the same occurs.

The following example will be used to match strings that represent single parameter mathematical functions:

regexp = r "[a-z] + (* [0-9] + *)"

This will find strings that start with one or more letters ([az] +), we have to escape the parentheses to take them as something we want to be part of the string, since the parentheses have a special meaning in regular expressions, we escape them with \, then we look for zero or more spaces (*) followed by numbers ([0-9] +) and again zero or more spaces.

Examples:

<u>Valid examples</u>

```
print re.findall(regexp,"cos(0)") == ["cos(0)"]

#>>> True

print  re.findall(regexp,"sqrt(    2       )")  ==
["sqrt( 2   )"]

#>>> True
```

<u>Invalid examples</u>

```
print re.findall(regexp,"cos    (0)") != ["cos    (0)"]

#>>> True

print re.findall(regexp,"sqrt(x)") != ["sqrt(x)"]

#>>> True
```

As we see, the first invalid example is precisely not
valid because we do not allow spaces between the
name of the function and the parentheses. The

second is wrong because the parameter is a letter instead of a number.

Let's see another one, this time we want to find strings that contain escape characters () and quotes

regexp = r '''(?: [^ \\] | (?: \.)) *'''

In this case, first we are going to look for chains that are enclosed in quotation marks (r '''''), what we find, we will find it zero or more times (r '''(? :) '''*), (? :) matches the regular expression in the parentheses. Next, we want anything other than a \, and note that we must escape it (r ''' (?: [^]) ''' *) Or (|) a. followed by any character (r ''' (?: [^ \] | (?:.)) ''' *)

Examples:

regexp = r '''(?: [^ \\] | (?: \.)) *'''

<u>Valid examples:</u>

```
print re.findall(regexp,'''I say, \"hello.\"''') == ['''I say, \"hello.\"''']
```

```
#>>> True
```

Invalid examples:

```
print re.findall(regexp,'"\"') != ['"\"']

#>>> True
```

Finally, a regular expression that will match all strings that are in double quotes:

regexp = r '"[^"] * "'

With this expression we look for chains that begin and end with (r '"'), cannot contain any character" between the string (r '"[^"]'), finally, we will consider the chain that meets this with any character zero or more times (r '"[^"] * "').

Examples:

Valid examples:

```
print re.findall(regexp,'"cuneiform"')
```

```
print re.findall(regexp,'"sumerian writing"')

print re.findall(regexp,'""')
```

Invalid examples

```
print re.findall(regexp,'"esc " ape"')
```

Chapter 5: Files & Error Handling In Python

Handling Exceptions in Python

Let's start with a simple program to add two numbers in Python. Our program takes two parameters as input and prints the sum. Here is a Python program to add two numbers:

```python
def addNumbers(a, b):

    print a + b



addNumbers (5, 10)
```

Try to run the previous Python program, and you should get the printed sum.

When writing the previous program, we don't really consider the fact that something could go wrong. What would happen if one of the last parameters is not a number?

```
addNumbers ('', 10)
```

We have not handled that case, therefore, our program will break with the following error message

```
Traceback (most recent call last):
  File "addNumber.py", line 4, in <module>
   addNumbers ('', 10)
  File "addNumber.py", line 2, in addNumbers
   print a + b
TypeError: cannot concatenate 'str' and 'int' objects
```

We can handle the above question by checking if the past parameters are integers. But that does not solve the problem. What happens if the code is broken for some other reason and causes the program to crash? Working with a program that breaks when encountering an error is not a good sight. Even if an unknown error has occurred, the code must be robust enough to handle the break with grace and that the user knows that something is wrong.

Exception Management Using Try and Except

In Python, we use the *try* and *except* statements to handle exceptions. When the code is broken, an exception occurs without the program crashing. We will modify the program that adds numbers to include the try and except statements.

```python
def addNumbers (a, b):
    try:
        return a + b
    except Exception as e:
        return 'Error occurred: ' + str(e)

print addNumbers ('', 10)
```

Python would process all the code within the try and except statements. When it finds an error, the control is passed to the except block, omitting the code in the middle.

As seen in the previous code, we have moved our code into a try and except statement. Try to run the program and you should throw an error message instead of the program crashing. Also, the reason for the exception is returned as an exception message.

The above method handles unexpected exceptions. Let's take a look at how to handle an expected exception. Assume we are trying to read a file with our Python program, but the file does not exist. In this case, we will control the exception and let the user know that the file does not exist when it occurs. Check out the file reading code:

```
try:
  try:
    with open('fname') as f:
      content = f. readlines ()
  except IOError as e:
    print str(e)
```

```
except Exception as e:
    print str(e)
```

In the previous code, we have handled the file reading within an IOError exception handler. If the code is broken due to the lack of availability of the fname file, the error would be handled within the IOError driver. Similar to the IOError exception, there are much more standard exceptions such as Arithmetic, OverflowError and ImportError, to name a few.

Multiple Exceptions

We can handle multiple exceptions at once by joining the standard exceptions as shown:

```
try:
    with open('fname') as f:
        content = f. readlines ()
    printb
except (IOError, NameError) as e:
    print str(e)
```

The above code would show the IOError and NameError exceptions when the program runs.

Clause finally

Suppose we are using certain resources in our Python program. During the execution of the program, an error was found and only executed halfway. In this case, the resource will be unnecessarily maintained. We can clean up such resources using the finally clause. Check out the following code:

```python
try:
    filePointer = open('fname','r')
    try:
        content = filePointer.readline()
    finally:
        filePointer.close()
except IOError as e:
    print str(e)
```

If during the execution of the previous code, an exception occurs when reading the file, filePointer would be closed in the finally block.

Logs in Python

When something goes wrong within an application, it is easier to debug if we know the source of the error. When an exception occurs, we can record the information necessary to locate the problem. Python provides a simple and powerful log library. Let's take a look at how to use Python records.

```python
import logging

# initialize the log settings
logging.basicConfig(filename='app.log',level=logging.INFO)

try:
    logging.info('Trying to open the file')
    filePointer = open('appFile','r')
    try:
```

```
    logging.info('Trying to read the file content')
    content = filePointer.readline()
finally:
    filePointer.close()
except IOError as e:
    logging.error('Error occurred ' + str(e))
```

As seen in the previous code, we first have to import the Python log library and then initialize the logger with the log file name and log level. There are five levels of registration: DEBUG, INFO, WARNING, ERROR and CRITICAL. Here we have to adjust the registration level to INFO; therefore, INFO and the previous records will be registered.

Getting Stack Tracking

In the previous code we had a program file, therefore it was easier to find out where the error had occurred. But what do we do when it comes to several program files? In such a case, getting the error stack helps in finding the source of the error.

The stack trace of the exception may have been recorded as shown:

```
import logging

# initialize the log settings
logging.basicConfig(filename = 'app.log', level = logging.INFO)

try:
    filePointer = open('appFile','r')
    try:
        content = filePointer.readline()
    finally:
        filePointer.close()
except IOError as e:
    logging.exception(str(e))
```

If you try to run the previous program, when an exception arises, the following error is recorded in the log file:

```
ERROR:root:[Errno 2] No such file or directory:
'appFile'
```

```
Traceback (most recent call last):
  File "readFile.py", line 7, in <module>
    filePointer = open('appFile','r')
IOError: [Errno 2] No such file or directory:
'appFile'
```

Chapter 6: Common Python Questions & Answers

1. What is the difference between list and tuples in Python?

Answer:

List Vs. Tuple	
List	**Tuples**
The lists are mutable, that is, they can be edited.	Tuples are immutable (tuples are lists that cannot be edited).
Lists are slower than tuples.	Tuples are faster than the list.
Syntax: list_1 = [10, 'Chelsea', 20]	Syntax: tup_1 = (10, 'Chelsea', 20)

2. What are the main features of Python?

Answer:

- Python is an interpreted language, contrary to other languages such as C and variants, Python does not need to be compiled before being executed. There are other interpreted languages such as PHP and Ruby.

- Python is written dynamically, this means that it is not necessary to indicate the types of variables when they are declared or something. You can do things like x = 111 and then x = "I am a string", without error.

- Python adapts very well to object-oriented programming because it allows classes to be defined along with composition and inheritance. It has no input specifiers (such as public, private C ++).

- In Python, functions are first-class objects. This means that they can be assigned to variables, returned from other functions and passed to functions. Classes are also first-class objects.

- Writing Python code is fast, but execution may be slower than compiled languages. Fortunately, Python allows you to include C-based extensions, so bottlenecks can be optimized and often are. The numpy package is a good example of this, is fast because most of the calculations that Python does not do.

- Python is useful in many areas: automation, web applications, large data applications, scientific modeling, and many more. It is also frequently used as an "intermediary" code to get other languages and components to play well.

3. What kind of language is Python? Programming or scripting?

Answer:

Python can create scripts, but, it is a general-purpose programming language.

4. How is Python interpreted?

Answer:

Python is an interpreted language, which is not in machine-level code before its runtime

5. What is Pep 8?

Answer:

PEP are acronyms that represent the Python Enhancement Proposal. And that specifies how to format the Python code so that it has maximum readability.

6. How is memory managed in Python?

Answer:

- Python memory is managed by Python private heap space. Then, Python data objects and structures are located in a private mound (a tree-like data structure).

The programmer has no entrance to this private mound, that is what the Python interpreter takes care of.

- The allocation of the space in mounds for Python objects is done by the Python memory manager. The main API gives input to several tools for the programmer to code.

- Python has a garbage collector included, which recycles the memory that is not in use and thus, can be made available to space in the mound.

7. What is namespace in Python?

Answer:

A namespace: is the name system used to ensure that names are unique and thus avoid name conflicts.

8. What is PYTHONPATH?

Answer:

It is an environment variable and is used when a module is imported. Also, PYTHONPATH is used to check the presence of imported modules in some directories. The interpreter uses it to determine which module to load.

9. What are Python modules? Name some of the built-in modules that are commonly used in Python?

Answer:

Python modules are files that have Python code. This code can be variables or classes of functions. A Python module is an .ly file that has executable code.

Some of the commonly used built-in modules are:

-JSON

-OS

-Random

-sys

-Data time

-Math

10. What are the main local and global variables in Python?

Answer:

Local variables:

It is the variable declared within a function. This variable is found in the local space and not in the global space.

Global Variables:

They are the variables declared outside a function or that are in the global space. These variables can be accessed from any function of the program.

Example:

```
a = 2                    #Variable Global

def add ():
```

```
b = 3                          #Variable Local

c = a + b

print (c)

add ()
```

Print: 5

When trying to enter the local variable outside the add () function, an error will occur.

11. Is Python case sensitive?

Answer:

Yes. Python is a language that is case sensitive.

12. What is Type Conversion in Python?

Answer:

Type conversion refers to the conversion of one type of data into another.

int () - convert any type of data into an integer type.

174

float () - convert any type of data into floating type.

ord () - convert characters to integers.

hex () - convert whole numbers to hexadecimal.

oct () - convert an integer to octal.

tuple () - This function is used to convert to a tuple.

set () - This function returns the type after converting it to set.

list () - This function is used to convert any type of data to a type of list.

dict () - This function is used to convert an ordered tuple (key, value) into a dictionary.

str () - Used to convert an integer into a string.

complex (real, imag) - This function converts real numbers into complex numbers (real, imag).

13. How to install Python on Windows and set a path variable?

Answer:

To install Python on Windows, follow the steps below:

- Install Python from this link: https://www.python.org/downloads/

- After that, install it on your PC. Find the location where Python was installed on your PC using the following command on the command line: cmd python.

- Next, go to the advanced system settings and add a new variable and name it as PYTHON_NAME and paste the copied path.

- Search for the route variable, select its value and select 'edit'.

- Add a semicolon after the value if it is not present and then type% PYTHON_HOME%.

14. Is indentation required in Python?

Answer:

Indentation is very necessary in Python. It specifies a block of code. All code within classes, functions, loops, etc., is specified within an indented block. Generally, it is done using four space characters. If your code is not indented, it will not be executed accurately and will throw errors.

15. What are Python functions?

Answer:

The function is a block of code that runs only when called. To define a function in Python, use the keyword def.

Example:

```
def Newfunction ():

print ("Hello, welcome")

New function (); #call the function
```

Print: Hello, welcome

16. What is a lambda function?

Answer:

An anonymous function is called a lambda function which can have different numbers of parameters but can have only one sentence.

Example:

```
a = lambda x, y: x + y

print (a (5, 6))
```

Print: 11

17. What is the Self in Python?

Answer:

The Self in Python is an instance or object of a class. It is explicitly included as the first parameter. However, in Java this is not the case, it is optional. This helps distinguish between methods and attributes of a class with local variables.

The variable self in the init method refers to the newly created object while in other methods, it refers to the object whose method was called.

18. What are the iterators in Python?

Answer:

The iterators in Python are objects that can be traversed or iterated.

19. How are comments written in Python?

Answer:

Comments in Python start with a # character. However, sometimes they alternate and comments are made using docstrings that are strings enclosed in triple quotes.

Example:

#The comments in Python start like this

print ("Comments in Python start with a #")

Output: Comments in Python start with #

20. What is pickling and unpickling?

Answer:

The Pickle module welcomes every Python object and transforms it into a string representation and sends it to a file using the dump function. This process is called pickling and the process of recovering original Python objects, from the stored string representation is called unpickling.

21. What are the generators in Python?

Answer:

Generators are the functions that return an iterable set of elements.

22. How is the first letter of a string capitalized?

Answer:

With the capitalize () method, capitalize the first letter of a string. But, if the string already has an uppercase letter at the beginning, then it returns the original string.

23. How do you convert the letters of a string to all lowercase?

Answer:

To convert a string to lowercase, use the lower () function.

Example:

```
stg='ABCD'

print(stg.lower())
```

Print: abcd

24. How can you comment on several lines in Python?

Answer:

The lines to comment must be preceded by a #. Then, the comments of several lines must have their # in each one. What needs to be done is to hold down the ctrl key, and click the left mouse button anywhere you want to include a # character, and type a # only once. This will comment on the selected lines with the cursor.

25. What is the use of the help () and dir () functions in Python?

Answer:

Help () and dir () are two functions accessible from the Python interpreter and are used to view a consolidated dump of built-in functions.

Help (): The help () function is used to present the documentation chain and makes it easy for you to see help related to modules, attributes, and keywords, etc.

Dir (): The dir () function is used to view the defined symbols.

26. When Python closes, why is not all allocated memory released?

Answer:

Whenever Python closes, especially Python modules that have circular references to other objects referred to from global namespaces, they are not always released.

It is difficult to deallocate the portions of memory that are reserved by the C library.

On leaving, by having its efficient cleaning mechanism, Python would try to deallocate/remove any other object.

27. What does this mean? * args, ** kwargs? And why would we use it?

Answer:

* Args is used when you are unsure of how many arguments are going to be passed to a function, or if you want to pass a list or tuple of saved arguments to a function.

** kwargs is used when we don't know how many keyword arguments are going to pass to a function, or it is used to pass the values of a dictionary as the keyword argument. The identifiers args and kwargs are a convention, you can also use * bob and ** billy but it would not be prudent.

28. What does len () do?

Answer:

It is used to determine the length of a list, matrix, string etc.

Example:

```
stg='ABCD'
len(stg)
```

29. What are Python programming packages?

Answer:

Namespaces that contain many modules are called packages.

30. Does Python have OOps concepts?

Answer:

Python is an object-oriented programming language. This means that any program can be solved in Python, creating an object model. However, Python can also be treated as procedural language and also as structural.

31. What are the Python libraries? Name some of them.

Answer:

Python libraries are the collection of Python packages. Among the most used libraries are Pandas, Matplotlib, Numpy, Scikit-learn, and many others.